The Brian Phillips Book of

Stuff That Rhymes

FOR MARIE

A brief look inside the mind of a well-seasoned

human being and part time folk singer.

Aimed to provide a modicum of amusement and

distraction from normality. It is my hope that a

number of charities will also benefit .

Publisher: Brian Phillips

Publication date: April 2020

ISBN: 978-1-78972-921-4

Author: Brian Phillips

Email: bphil.21@live.co.uk

Address: Brian Phillips

21 Willow Close

Bedworth

Warwickshire

England

CV12 8BE

Please direct all enquiries to the author.

Artwork and Production:
Adrian Jones
adri@n10net.com of
Cornwall Folk Festival
www.CornwallFolkFestival.com

Contents

AND SO IT BEGINS

The idea of this book of poems and nonsense all began about two years ago following an impromptu story that I invented one evening about a wayward Whelk named Roger. This later prompted kind members of the audience to ask for more detail about some of the characters that had materialised throughout the tale and I had little choice but to respond. The subsequent interest reached a level that seemed to cry out for a book.

So here it is! Based on factual fiction (I made it up, but I really did). Thoughts on our wonderful world, our bodies and some of the beautiful creatures that we share this mad planet with. The only intention is to amuse you and maybe  provoke thought. I have enjoyed writing and preparing this work and I truly hope that it will raise the odd smile here and there.

My sincere thanks to Katrina and Donna Dalton for freely giving their time and talent to produce such wonderful drawings. Thank you.

BRIAN

ROGER THE WHELK

This is the story of Roger the Whelk

which is not as depraved as it seems

It's simply the tale of a seagoing snail

and the things about which he dreams

He lies on his seabed each evening

Thinking of new things to do

Like wandering around on the wet salty ground

in search of something new to stick to

In the absence of anything special

He would stick to a rock round or flat

But a real delight would be to stumble one
    night

On a rug or a whelkoming mat

Oh, how happy Roger was

Paddling around on the ocean floor

Until one day storm and tempest struck

And he got washed up on the shore

It changed his life that stormy day

To leave his briny home

And find himself in the open air

With a sandy beach to comb

He explored the local area

And found a place to stay

He stuck himself to a boulder

On the east side of the bay

The boulder was ideally placed

Where the water ebbed and flowed

So, he was sometimes wet and sometimes
   dry

The perfect whelk abode

All was good for Roger

Until one fateful day

A mussel moved in next to him

And said "I'm here to stay"

Roger said "oh no you're not,

For this is my domain"

And he hit the mussel with a nearby stone

And then he hit it once again

And so, the fight had started

Bits of shell flying everywhere

And a mucus like trail of destruction

Left the smell of death in the air

The mussel struck next with a powerful
	blow

But the whelk dodged away from the tussle

He tore that mollusc off the rock

Yes! Roger had pulled a mussel

Roger was full of anger now

A raging deadly shell

And the mussel taunted Roger

This was the shellfish fight from hell

But then fate intervened again

And a shocking thing occurred

As Roger prepared for the killer blow

He got picked up by a bird

The bird said "hello Roger

How's it hanging mate"

Roger said "I'm good thanks Hmmm" (it
      was a humming bird)

"Drop me off at Billingsgate"

"Sorry I can't do that "

Said Hmm to the airborne whelk

"I'm taking you to Sweden

It's the land of the bloated Elk"

"Ah Sweden" Rog thought to himself

"I've got friends who live there

Gordon Rameses the Egyptian chef

And Olga the elk dragger fair"

They flew out over the sprawling sea

Roger and the seagull

If they'd flown over the bay instead

It would've been a bay gull

Through rain and shine and wind and calm

They travelled over the sea and Norway

Then the keen-eyed gull saw Olga's house

And dropped Roger off at the doorway.

Olga squealed with joy when she saw Rog

And Joy squealed as well

The prodigal whelk was home again

As into her arms he fell

The circle of love was complete once more

Olga couldn't believe her luck

"You won't leave me again will you Rog"

And he said "No"

WHAT HAPPENED TO THE MUSSEL?

After the fight with Roger the Whelk

Darcy Mussel withdrew into his shell

He never went out; he was full of self-
    doubt

He was living a life of sheer hell

But then one day his shell phone rang

And it was the BBC

"What we want to do is to interview you"

And he said "Do what? To who? To me"?

So, on the day a crew turned up

At Darcy Mussels' home

A crab with a camera a prawn with some
    lights

And a squid armed with 8 microphones

The reporter Nellie was a jelly fish

And she didn't mess about

She started questioning straight away

Determined not to leave anything out

"So! Darcy" she said, "who threw the first
   punch?

Who landed the first blow?

Was it Roger or you who was the rogue of
   the two

The viewers are so keen to know"

"It was that bastard Roger he started the
   fight

He just went berserk" said Darce

"He went for my shell like a Whelk out of
   hell

And knocked me clean on my arse"

"But didn't you steal his rock?" said Nellie.

"Didn't you encroach on his land?

It was you you rotter you bivalvial squatter

You should have remained in the sand."

"Oh, so suddenly I'm the baddie" Darcy
    retorted

"I thought this was supposed to fair

Impartial my arse" said the affronted Darce

And he pushed Nellie right off her chair

Well that did it another fight started

Before you could say cephalopod

Nellie lashed out with her sting at the rage
    encrazed thing

But she missed and pollacksed a cod

All the time the camera was rolling

Filming these new altercations

The octopus threw eight left hooks fast and
true

And knocked out eight nearby crustaceans

This triggered a bloody pitched battle

With fish and other marine life too
numerous to mention

The way it was going with blood and guts
flowing

Some of these wouldn't live to draw pension

Crowds gathered in their thousands as the
word spread

They were queuing in droves just to see 'em

The sea bed was bright red with the blood
being shed

Like a sell out at Rome's colosseum

It was obvious that Darcy was unpopular

As the whole crew waded in to the fray

Biting and punching pinching and crunching

Darcy was having a bad day

Oh, it was awful the carnage and gore

And all caused by a news media wannabe star

Nellie should be ashamed, she'll surely be
blamed

The scene looked a like a Sushi Bar

Darcy tried to escape from the bloodthirsty
mob

But his aggressors had got other plans

Then with one desperate leap he wound up in
a heap

Of carelessly discarded plastic bottles and
cans

The oysters didn't really get involved

They were out with their father Merle

There was the brother of Barry, the sister of
    Larry

And of course, Lily the mother of Pearl

Never before had such slaughter been
    known

All because of jellyfish Nellie

Fatally wounded were lying

Sons and daughters were dying

They could never show this on the telly.

Even a rock band was set up

With drums and guitars strumming

"Come on everyone join in with the fun"

And the sperm whale shouted "I'm coming"

Then an eerie silence enveloped the scene

As the word spread that Darcy had died

He was knocked into a vat of boiling hot
fat

Darcy Mussel had been deep fat fried

Darcy was hounded by the news hungry
press

They were responsible for his untimely
demise

Nellie, her crew and the rest of them too

With their saline smorgasbord of fake news
and lies

Will they be held to bear for the things that
they did?

The hounding of innocent sea life

The relentless prying as Darcy lay dying

Showing no respect or regard for his wife

No, they'll survive to do it again

After all that's what sells the papers we buy

And perhaps we all share the blame for this
      cheap nasty game

It's us who creates the demand and supply

Farewell Darcy your life was too short

But you certainly made your mark

Poems and tales of whelks seagulls and
      whales

But no mention yet of a shark!

IBBLE THE GULL

Some of you may remember

The flight of Hmm the gull

With Roger the whelk

To the land of the Elk

And how he flew back home to Hull

Much had happened while Hmm was away

And things were far from great

His territory invaded, his nests all were
        raided

By a bird he once thought was his mate

All the haunts where Hmm used to fly

Were now flown by this young pretender

And so, Hmm duly swore to settle the
score

By challenging Ibble to go on a bender

They met in Gullivers bar at eight

And the drinking binge began

The other gulls were in awe at the sight that
they saw

As they guzzled beer can after can

Soon the beer had run out

And spirits were suggested

With points being gained for each glass that
was drained

And the skill with which they were ingested

By ten o clock Hmm and Ibble were pissed

But neither bird would give in

Ibble said "right ex mate let's escalate

Barman crack open some bottles of gin"

"You bastard" Hmm thought to himself

(As there was no one else he could think to)

"He knows I hate gin now he'll probably win

Unless I can find new depths to sink to"

And so, it was that Hmm put super glue

On the rim of young Ibble's glass

And when his beak touched the edge of
that adhesive laced ledge

Hmm knew that he'd nailed Ibble's ass

But Ibble sensed that there was still a slight
gap

Into which he could insert a straw

So, he continued to sip through the hole in
his lip

And the contest ended a draw

To decide which one would be winner

Stunt flying was organised over the bay

The public were told and tickets were sold

It promised to be a great day

It started well with Hmm

Doing triple rolls upside down

While Ibble climbed high to the roof of the
    sky

Playing a trumpet while dressed as a clown

Next Ibble dived deep into the ocean

With a dazzling show of power

So, Hmm said "screw you" and he did it too

And didn't come up for an hour

Hmm was desperate to win the day

And be top gull once and for all

So, he said "right Ibble let's end this quibble

With a suicide flight into the wall"

Both birds had to fly at top speed

Towards the harbour wall

But just in time do a vertical climb

And the surviving gull would take all

They flew neck and neck towards the hard
   stone

Neither one was prepared to give way

And at the end of the run Hmm shot up
   towards the sun

But poor Ibble had lived his last day

They scraped Ibble up from the foot of the
    wall

And buried him near to the shore

Hmm said a few words to all of the birds

And laid a plaque in the shape of a claw

Here lies what's left of gull Ibble

In defeat may he forever rest

With this wall he collided and thus it was
        decided

Of all gulls Hmm is the best

FLATULENCE

Don't start me on flatulence

It can be really funny at the start

But once you get past sixty

You must never trust a fart

Now I know it classed as impolite

To simply let one go

Even if it's a quiet one

Or you're with someone you know

But sometimes you just can't help yourself

It has to be set free

You just hope that it is a silent one

And completely odour free

Well good luck with that then

Cos that's not what life is like

You know it's gonna stink like hell

And sound like a motor bike

The problem is that once it's out

It's too late to try to smother

And any sudden movements

May instigate another

We've all tried many different ways

To cover up this antisocial act

Of emitting foul toxic gas

From our unmentionable tract

My favourite method without a doubt

Is the innocent third party blame

Just sidle up real close to them

And release that cloud of shame

And when the deed is done don't run away

Just look at them and grin

Then in a loud accusing voice

Say "good for you better out than in"

I tried to light one up one day

Following advice from an old school chum

But it didn't end well, and I finished up

With 3rd degree burns to my bum

And if you stick a duck caller

Firmly in the crack

Every time you need to fart

Your bum goes quack quack quack

Anyway, that's all there is

Of farts I'll say no more

May all your farts be deadlier

Than the fart that came before

And each night when you go to sleep

Your body will make more gas

So that the minute that you wake up again

You can blow it out your ass

AH! SOLE

Ah Sole! My favourite fish

I eat it every day

It would be made compulsory

If I had my milky way

Ooh! Milky Way a lovely snack

A really smashing chocolate treat

Eating more than a dozen though

Would surely be no mean feat

My feet and shoes are really mean to me

They won't do as they're told

When I take them for repair

First, they're heeled and then are soled

Ah Sole! my favourite fish

I eat it every day

It would be made compulsory

If I had my Milky Way

SNOT

And Snot, who on earth invented that?

I mean what does it do

It lives up your nose and it won't come
down

It starts off really runny and is

Impossible to stop

And then it goes quite glutinous

Like the fat on a cold pork chop

After that comes the blockage stage

When nothing moves at all

Your head feels like a bag of glue

Or a jelly filled basketball

You blow and blow til you ears pop

But alas it's to no avail

Then out it comes like ectoplasm

Or the contents of a snail

It's a horrible thought that we're walking
    round

With a head full of germ filled goo

Don't get too near to me my dear

Or you might get it too

EARWAX

Why do we have earwax?

I really don't know why

Is my cranium a candle factory?

That's become redundant from years gone
by

So, in the event of a power cut

When I need a light to shine

I can stick a wick in each ear hole

And burn brightly til about half past nine

Perhaps it's there to set a trap

For unwelcome bugs and flies

When they get stuck in that aural muck

It facilitates their demise

Or maybe it's for furniture

To bring it to a shine

You'd need a lot but it's at least it's free

That's how I'm going to use mine

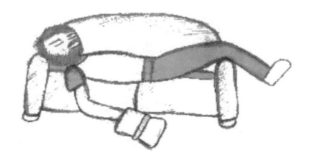

IT'S HAPPENING AGAIN

My head tilts back into the chair

I sit there dozing without a care

I dream of days when all was right

And troubled times were out of sight

My mind takes me to a better place

Where the world is easier to face

Where good things happen, never bad

Where happy never turns to sad

I wander through leafy glades and lanes

No noise from cars or aeroplanes

Just the peace of the countryside

A tranquil feeling deep inside

I'm taken along a sandy beach

The ocean just within my reach

Seagulls soaring overhead

I wonder what next lies ahead

I start to rise and try to wake

There are other journeys yet to make

My eyes ease open with a gentle rub

I'm pissed; I'd dropped off in the pub

MICE LOVERS

I found two dead mice on the lawn last
  night

Lying together cold and still

Were they murdered in their sleep?

Or had they just been ill

Were they scared to death by a cat?

Or was old age the cause

But they both looked quite young

And no bites or marks from claws

And then I realised the awful truth

They hadn't been attacked

These two rodent lovers

Had made a suicide pact

Their folks had told them "you're too
        young

We will not let you wed"

So, they ran away together

And now are sadly dead

ODE TO AN UNWANTED SPOT

I was living blissfully just beneath your skin

With not a single care

I felt safe and I felt warm

Where I was nestled near your hair

All was well for me and the others

We didn't feel under threat

But then you met your brother's mate

And the tragic scene was set

You started taking notice

Of the way that you appeared

And you explored ways in which

Your complexion could be cleared

At first it was just gentle soap

With water barely hot

And then you tried astringents

Which did tend to sting a lot

In desperation though one day

Before your first real date

In order to look perfect

For your bloody brother's mate

You lined me up against the mirror

With a finger on either side

And squeezed til I erupted

On a fast and deadly ride

I splattered on the mirror

And slid towards the floor

Leaving a crater in your face

Which I hoped was really sore

I was wiped up with a tissue

And discarded in the loo

May the spots of a thousand trolls

Now come and live on you

So next time you see a spot or boil

And think "that's got to go"

Spare a thought for us blemishes

We have a life as well you know

Cover us up with make up

And we'll soon go if you just wait

Then we can briefly live together

And sod your brother's mate

I'M STAYING SINGLE

I'm staying single til I meet my double

Then I'll marry myself for sure

I'm staying single til I find my double

And I'll look for love no more.

I'll be so very happy

Just me and me alone

I won't even have to change my name

I'll be like my own clone

Of course, there'll be no babies

That could never be

I just can't imagine myself

Doing that to me

We'll just grow old together

Sharing clothes and playing guitar

Mr and Mr Brian Phillips

Hip op hip op hoorah.

And when it's time to give it up

I'll go and not complain

Because as we all know if to church we go

We'll be coming back again.

LORENZO

Lorenzo the centipede could walk very fast

Four minutes to cover one mile

He was arrested, because bugs he'd
      molested

He was a centipedofile

SWEATISH FETISH (For Maria)

When I'm on stage I get quite hot

At least that's what I'm told

So I need a cloth to wipe me down

A small one that's easy to fold

I've seen other performers doing this

And I want to do the same

To stop me from getting soaking wet

Perspiration is of course to blame

This has also brought about

A most unfortunate fetish

I just love to look at people

As they become increasingly sweatish

There's one case in particular

That simply drives me wild

At the end of her act it's a humid fact

Her neckerchief is defiled

I can't stop thinking about that rag

It will be on my epitaph

I'm begging you Maria PLEASE

Give me your sweaty scarf.

PYRAMIDS EXPLAINED

If I'd been born in Egypt

There is one thing I'd resent

Millions of tons of golden sand

And not one bag of cement

That's why it's always been believed

Pyramids were so difficult to construct

With nothing to stick the blocks together

You were basically out of luck

Experts say how brilliant

That they were interlinked so tight

But actually, it didn't matter

If one of them wasn't right

As long as the one next to it

Was adjusted to ensure a fit

They just carried on building

Block by block and nobody gave it a
        second thought

And it's obvious to me why

They were pointed at the top

Just keep building upwards at an angle

Until there's one block left then stop

Blocks were dragged all the way up ONE
     side

Very slowly brother alongside brother

And when they got to the required spot

They slid on their arses down the other

So that's my theory of how they were built

These monolithic follies

Only to be gawped at thousands of years
     later

By tourists on their jollies

SUPERIOR PEOPLE

I detest superior people

They bloody know it all

How the universe was made

Why are atoms small

Why is the sky up there?

Why is the sea blue and green?

Why does stuff grow in the ground?

Why can God be mean?

How do we know when to wake up?

How do we know when to sleep?

How do we know when to sow?

How do we know when to reap?

Who decides when we are born?

Who chooses when we die?

Who keeps us well or makes us ill?

Who's really behind our eye?

KUALA LUMPUR

I went out with a girl from Kuala Lumpur

And she kept stolen goods up her jumper

I told her one night this isn't right

And I decided right then that I'd dump her

MONK

I once knew a monk who was way
    overweight

To slim was his one desire

He'd sit on his own and meditate

He was a deep fat friar

UNFORTUNATE WALTER

Walter was unfortunate

To say the very least

For he was born with a wonky willy

A really unruly beast

It didn't matter too much

When Walter was just a child

But as he matured much strife he endured

With a willy that had gone totally wild

Doctors said it was probably

Caused by some prenatal infection

That sadly meant it was not only bent

But would unexpectedly change its direction

For instance, Walter would stand at the
    urinal

Waiting for the urge to do it

But when it finally came it was such a shame

Cos he weed in the urinal next to it

The situation was grim for our Walter

The poor man could hardly cope

He could be out round the shops when pfff
    out it pops

Looking around like a live periscope

Walter said perhaps it's possessed

The spirit must be driven away

But Willy heard Wally and made him pay
     for his folly

By giving his Y fronts a spray

Well Walter finally found a solution

To keep Willy from going astray

He strapped the poor guy to the inside of
     his thigh

And that's where he's destined to stay

TRIBUTE TO THE COMMON COLD

Oh, to be a bogey

Living up a nose

Oblivious of what might happen

Next time the hooter blows

You might stay up there for days or weeks

Without seeing the light of day

But sooner or later you will fly out

And there'll be hell to pay

Germs all neatly bundled up

In that bead like ball of yack

It might land in someone's drink

Or stick to a person's back

Regardless of where it does end up

One thing is for sure

This alienesque chunk of stretchy gunk

Will dwell in me no more

I like the thought that now it's gone

I'm free of that viscose clod

And that something that's been living in me

Now lives in some other poor sod.

GASEOUS CLAY

Let me tell you about Gaseous Clay

The well-known flatulent fighter

He wouldn't have been as good as he was

If his bum had been a bit tighter

But as it was with a bottom so loose

He was able to create sheer hell

Because every time he threw a punch

A fart came out as well

Imagine how difficult it would be

To combat this invisible toxin

Fighting his arse as well as his fists

It's a funny way to go BOXIN'

No one could ever beat him

He was the ultimate fighter

Until one night under the ring lights bright

His opponent produced a fag lighter

As Gaseous threw a left hook then a right

The other guy ignited the jet

And a big blue flash preceded a loud crash

And his arse became crap Suzette

The ring looked like an oil field

With Gaseous Clay lying flat on his face

And a twenty-foot flume lit up the room

As his arse blasted gas into space

No one could get close to help him

So, sprinklers were set off in the arena

Water lapped around the fire, but the
    flames just grew higher

His arse had never been cleaner

His friend Red Adair was in the audience

He said "I'll stop him from being alight

Get my fireproof gear and four pints of
    beer

Oh, and two sticks of dynamite"

Red suited up and approached the blaze

The heat almost too much to bear

He guzzled his beer as he edged his way
    near

Whilst inhaling the stench of bum hair

Finally, Red was at the source of the fire

And he readied the dynamite

He prised open the hole with a large metal
    pole

And then rammed the sticks in real tight

Red scurried away from the ring

And turned once just to say goodbye

Farewell old chum and Farewell old chums
    bum

The end is about to be nigh

Suddenly there was a deafening bang

Then it became cold and dark

As quick as it started, his last fart was farted

Beaten all because of a spark

Men will try to emulate him

In the years to come

The speed of his hands and his anal glands

That empowered that infamous bum

But none will equal Gaseous Clay

Never mind surpass his achievement

He truly excelled and all others he out
    smelled

Without doubt boxing's greatest
    bereavement

LIFE UNDER MY ARMS

What goes on under my arms?

I'd really love to know

What wildlife might dwell in this tropical
dell?

What grotesque things might grow?

Armpits are intriguing things and are largely
unexplored

Who knows what lies concealed?

All caked and congealed

What wondrous things are stored?

I think it's a microscopic world

Like the land that time forgot

With miniature dinosaurs and terrible
    dactyls

Patrolling through sweat sodden grot

Imagine an eco-system under your arms

Providing food and warmth for creatures

Things with horns and wings and spiky
    things

And many more interesting features

So next time you get an itch

Suppress that urge to scratch

It's probably some previously unknown
    species

Wriggling around in its efforts to hatch

Crikey! New flora and fauna under my very
own arms

Things all named after me

The Bri-tosaurus and the Philliraptor

And the flying Whelk to name but three

Books will be written about the new world

"The oxter a new beginning"

I'll become a famous authorage

And many prizes I'll be winning

I'll be awarded the Attenborough Trophy

And the David Bellamy pwize for
pwehistoric wesearch

My name will be on mugs and plates

And on a plaque in my hometown church

SOCK

A lone sock lies in my bedside drawer

Pining for its other

They'd been walking side by side so long

They'd fallen for each other

I can't bear to throw it way

In case its mate returns

Only to find it's been abandoned

By the one for which it yearns

So, I keep it in the corner

Where its survival is assured

Until sock 2 comes back one day

And the union is restored

But hang on a bit I've had a thought

What sex is the sock that's missing?

And what sex is the remaining one

What genders have been kissing?

These socks will go on either foot

No preference left or right

And after a wash they may swap sides

And try that for a night

Where's this going what have I done

Bisexual socks that's stupid

It makes me feel like a sock demi god

A sort of sock drawer Cupid

Oh no now I'm thinking discrimination

What about different colours and types?

We don't wear one black one and one
    white one

Or one plain and one with stripes

We should treat all socks as equals

That's what equality's all about

So, socks wouldn't be discarded

But would be kept until worn out

Sockiatric wards in hospitals

For socks that need repairing

Damaged by their human host

Victims of abusive wearing

And finally, a sock care home

Where worn out socks could be put

When they are no longer well enough

To adorn a human foot

END

(My sincere thanks for entering my world for a little while)

About The Author

Brian Phillips

Brian Phillips was born in 1950 to parents Milly and Harold and has an older brother John. His father was a Royal Marines commando in World War II and, after demob, he worked in a coal mine near Coventry. A serious mining accident changed his father's and the family's lives forever. Despite this, Harold still managed to be a wonderful hard-working father and lived to a good age. Brian's mother was a remarkable lady and strove hard all her working life to help support Brian and John.

Brian went to comprehensive school in Bedworth followed by an apprenticeship at G.E.C. Telecommunications and then a spell in the Coventry and Warwickshire Constabulary. He married his darling Marie in 1976 and they had four wonderful children – Shelley, Donna, Brian and Rebecca – who blessed them with ten super grandchildren.

Brian and Marie then ran a lovely village pub in the Vale of Evesham, after which he spent a long time in marine fire protection, travelling extensively. During this period Marie obtained a Certificate of Education in Computer Information and Technology and taught for several years at a local college.

Brian and Marie next ran a successful photographic studio in a village neighbouring Bedworth. Holidays were always spent in their beloved Padstow, Cornwall, where they made many good friends; Brian still visits at least once a year. In 2009 they retired from the business due to health issues affecting them both. Sadly in 2014 Marie lost her courageous battle with cancer and left a space in the family that can never be filled.

Marie Phillips

Throughout their courtship and marriage Brian and Marie shared a common love of folk (and other) music and performed mainly as a duo in folk clubs and festivals right up until Marie's illness made it impossible for her to continue. They were fortunate to record a CD 'Living Legacy' in 2014. After a short break Brian kept his promise to Marie and continues to perform locally and further afield.

In recent years, driven by some unknown force, Brian has taken to writing humorous poetry and feels that now is the time to share some of it with you.